# THE CIGAR IN ART

# THE CIGAR IN ART

## introduction by Terence Conran

The Overlook Press
Woodstock • New York

First published in 1996 by
The Overlook Press
Lewis Hollow Road
Woodstock, New York  12498

**Library of Congress Cataloging-in-Publication Data**

The cigar in art / introduction by Terence Conran.
128p. 18.5cm.
1. Cigars in art. I. Conran, Terence. II. Overlook
Press.
N8253. T6C54  1996
704.9'4967972—dc20
96-36338
CIP

ISBN: 0-87951-693-3
Printed in England by
BAS Printers Limited
Over Wallop, Hampshire
First Edition

**Editor**
Tracy Carns

**Research and Project Management**
John and Ann Taylor,
John Taylor Book Ventures

**Additional Research**
Steven Anderson
Hermann Lademann

**Design**
Michael Hornburg
Tracy Carns
Malcolm Preskett

# Sometimes a cigar is just a cigar

Sigmund Freud

# Introduction

**W**hen I'm drinking tea at breakfast, I'm looking forward with keen anticipation to my first cup of very strong Gourmet Noir coffee and my first Hoyo de Monterrey Epicure No. 2 cigar. For me, that's the true start of the day. The coffee and cigar work wonders, sending adrenaline pulsing through my veins. If I'm honest, only Cuban cigars will really do, which presents a problem every time I visit the United States: I have to pass through Customs and Immigration with an open box, promising that my cigars are purely for personal consumption (and they are!)

It's difficult to be bad-tempered with a good cigar in one's mouth. (Freud, no doubt, had something to say about that.) The very best way to enjoy a cigar is sitting in a large, comfortable wicker chair in the greenhouse, a large glass of Calvados to one side, a good book to the other, and nobody within earshot to corrupt the experience. Of course, you shouldn't smoke a cigar when you're talking to other people, or writing or drawing, or involved in any other distraction, yet I somehow seem to manage.

Cigars in paintings and other works of art—the subject of the book at hand—represent gloriously, in little more than a brush stroke, the pure joy of smoking a cigar, a joy that is often shown in art as an indulgence of the rich, in paintings like Diego Rivera's "Night of the Rich." Like many luxuries, cigars have acquired vulgar connotations of status. You know perfectly well that you should *never* agree to be photographed cigar in hand for the business pages unless you want to be branded a capitalist pig. It's quite unjust really—you wonder what the *Wall Street Journal* would make of Fidel Castro.

But cigars in art have also signified an attainable pleasure that transcends class, in paintings like Edward Hopper's "Sunday" or Edward Burra's "Harlem." It seems cigars in art represent not merely a rich life, but a life richly lived, irrespective of one's tax bracket.

Cigars carry all sorts of connotations and associations. For me, they are to maturity what the cigarette once was to teenagers: fashion accessory, symbol of independence, at times louchely decadent. I smoked my first cigar (a Romeo y Julietta) aged 32, and have worked up gradually to my current diet of four cigars a day. Along with fine Burgundies, cigars are my single greatest indulgence.

Of the sensory pleasures associated with cigars, the tactile are often overlooked. There's something distinctly fetishistic about the rituals of cigar-smoking. I get a real thrill opening the cedarwood box and tugging the yellow ribbon with which the cigars are tied in bundles of 25 or 50. The outer cigars have a slightly bruised indention from the ribbon, which perhaps adds to the pleasure of rolling the fine cigar between your thumb and forefinger while you anticipate the delicious pleasures of lighting up.

Lighting the cigar should take a long time in itself, a chance to savor the quality of the finest, hand-rolled Havana. Ideally, I like to use spills from the cedarwood membrane that separates the layers of cigars in their box. You should always warm the barrel, then roll the cigar to ensure it's lit properly and evenly at the end. Again, Freud might have something to say about this prenuptial preparation.

Cigars inspire devotion. I swear by their Sybaritic pleasures, and, because one never inhales, I can lull myself into believing they are doing me no harm whatsoever.

TERENCE CONRAN

He sat at the Algonquin, smoking a cigar.

A coffin of a clock bonged out the time.

She was ten minutes late.  But in that time,

He puffed the blue eternity of his cigar.

—Howard Moss, "At The Algonquin"

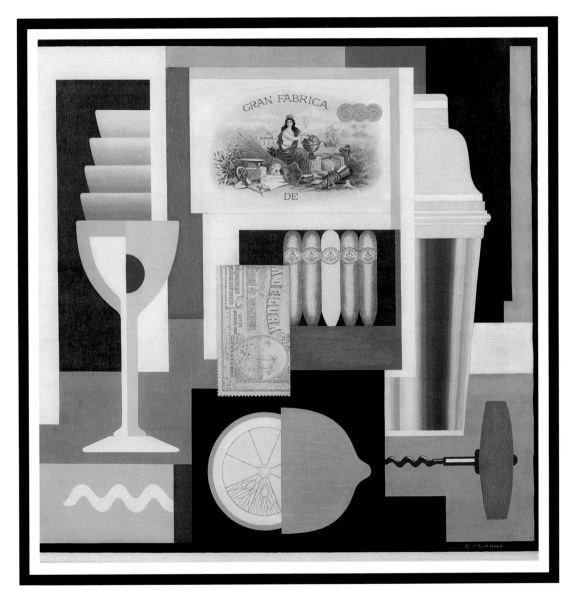

**COCKTAIL**
BY GERALD
MURPHY

The *light* ones may be killers,
  And the *dark* ones may be mild;
Not the **wrappers** but the *fillers*,
Make cigars or women *wild*.

—Keith Preston, *Popular Fallacies*

**VEGAS BLACKJACK**
BY LEROY NEIMAN

**MONEY IS LIKE A SIXTH SENSE, WITHOUT WHICH YOU CANNOT MAKE USE OF THE OTHER FIVE.**

**W. SOMERSET MAUGHAM**

THE DUKE AND DUCHESS OF WINDSOR IN MADISON SQUARE GARDEN
BY WEEGEE (DETAIL)

# No, not rich. I am a poor man with money, which is not the same thing.

Gabriel García Márquez,
*Love in the Time of Cholera*

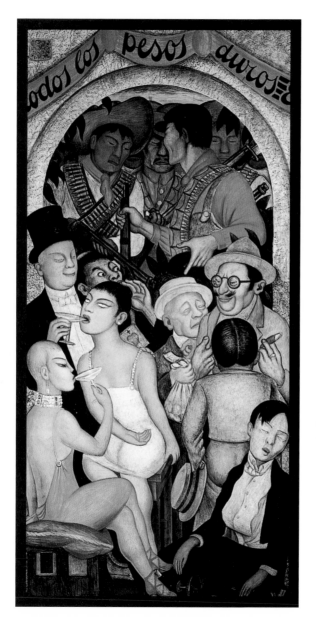

**THE NIGHT OF
THE RICH**
BY DIEGO RIVERA

# Pull out a Montecristo
at a dinner party, and the political liberal turns into the nicotine fascist.

Martyn Harris

**PRIVATE VIEW**
BY BERYL COOK

Yes, social friend, I *love* thee well,
In learned doctors' spite;
Thy *clouds* all other *clouds* dispel,
And lap me in delight.

*CHARLES SPRAGUE, "To My Cigar"*

ENNUI
BY WALTER
SICKERT

# IT IS NOW PROVED BEYOND A SHADOW OF A DOUBT THAT SMOKING IS ONE OF THE LEADING CAUSES OF STATISTICS

Fletcher Knebel, *Reader's Digest,* 12/(

**MEN WITH CIGARS**
BY MILTON GLASER

# When Freud met Mahler

They were Jews by birth (unreligious, but puritanical) and Viennese by adoption. Freud had been a medical student in Vienna when Mahler was at the conservatory. Later Mahler served as conductor of the Vienna Court Opera. Opera was one of Freud's few diversions. But they did not meet until Freud was fifty-four and Mahler, at fifty, had less than a year to live.

The encounter was occasioned by the composer's marital problems with the young and beautiful Alma. Engrossed in his Tenth Symphony, Mahler suddenly found himself the object of domestic rebellion. Alma had, she said, submitted to his tyranny and neglect long enough; she felt used, drained by his self-absorption. The truth of her accusations, together with a case of impotence, produced in Mahler both guilt and panic—panic that was not eased by the appearance of another man (Walter Gropius) on the scene. Immediate action was called for.

Freud, vacationing in Leyden, Holland, that summer of 1910, received a telegram asking for an appointment. The following day came another telegram, canceling. Mahler's vacillation was repeated twice more before he managed to conquer his resistance.

*He and Freud met in a Leyden hotel and spent the next four hours strolling about the town—the stocky, confident doctor and the thin, intense composer—smoking the cigars both adored. Freud conducted a sort of mini-analysis. A mother fixation was diagnosed:*

Mahler was attracted by his wife's youthful beauty but resented that she was not old and careworn like his mother. Alma, to even things out, had a father complex and found her husband's age appealing. Mahler was reassured.

The two men parted friends. Mahler's potency returned, and psychoanalysis got the credit. Alma said later that Freud had reproached her husband for marrying one so young, but his attitude was closer to sympathy than to censure. A good wife—in Freud's view as in Mahler's—was but a ministering angel put on earth for the comfort and support of her husband.

**Nancy Caldwell Sorel**

**MEETING OF FREUD AND MAHLER**
BY EDWARD SOREL

**People smoke for their mental health, don't they?  It's part of their total health, I'd say.**

# David Hockney

**VILLA REALE, MARLIA**
BY DAVID HOCKNEY

"And a woman is only a woman, but a good cigar is a smoke."
—Rudyard Kipling, *The Betrothed*

**AT THE BAR**
BY STRIBRNY (DETAIL)

"When I don't smoke, I scarcely feel as if I'm living." RUSSELL HOBAN

PORTRAIT OF NORMAN DOUGLAS
BY MICHAEL AYRTON

If alcohol is queen, then tobacco is her consort. It's a fond companion for all occasions, a loyal friend through fair weather and foul. People smoke to celebrate a happy moment, or to hide a bitter regret. Whether you're alone or with friends, it's a joy for all the senses. **Luis Buñuel**

CHICA IN A BAR
BY RAMON CASAS

Nothing great was ever achieved without ENTHUSIASM

—Ralph Waldo Emerson

ASPECTS OF URBAN LIFE: GOLF
BY PAUL CADMUS

A portrait is a picture in which there is a little something that is not quite right about the mouth.

John Singer Sargent

ASHER WERTHEIMER
BY JOHN SINGER SARGENT
(DETAIL)

"What this country needs is a *really good* five-cent cigar."

–Vice-president T.R. Marshall,

*New York Tribune*, Jan. 4, 1920

**THE OPERA BUFF**
BY L. VAN DE GHENST

*Our country has plenty of good* **five-cent cigars,** *but the trouble is they charge* **fifteen cents** *for them.*

# Will Rogers

**SUNDAY**
BY EDWARD
HOPPER
(DETAIL)

"Fortunes come tumbling into some men's laps."

—Francis Bacon

**CITY LIFE**
DETAIL OF THE
MURAL "AMERICA
TODAY" BY THOMAS
HART BENTON

# There is no wealth but Life.

**John Ruskin**

**HARLEM**
BY EDWARD BURRA

"It is not enough
to conquer;
one must know how
to seduce."
VOLTAIRE

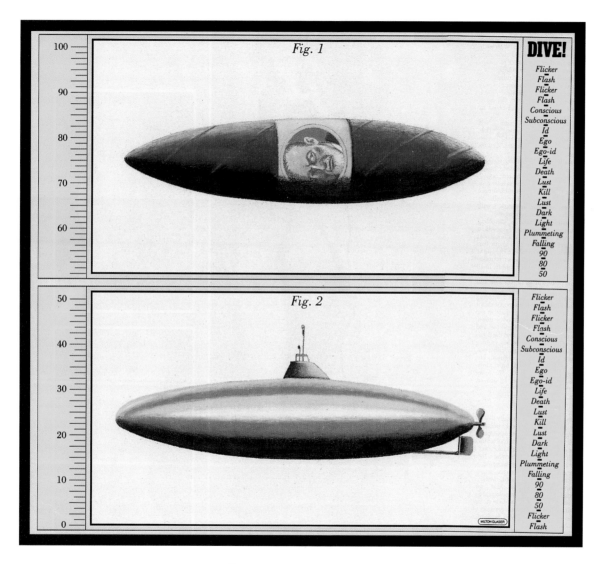

**THESE ARE NOT CIGARS**
BY MILTON GLASER

# We must never confuse elegance with snobbery.

## Yves Saint Laurent

FASHION PLATE
BY PIERO FORNASETTI

MAN IS A CREATION OF $\text{DESIRE}$, NOT A CREATION OF NEED.

GASTON BACHELARD

**CHICAGO DUTCH MASTERS**
BY LARRY RIVERS
(DETAIL)

"In matters of grave importance, **style,** not sincerity, is the **vital** thing."

—Oscar Wilde,

*The Importance of Being Earnest*

FUMEUR A L'EPÉE
BY PABLO PICASSO

**T**obacco is a dirty weed: I like it.
It satisfies no normal need: I like it.
It makes you thin, it makes you lean,
It takes the hair right off your bean;
It's the worst darn stuff I've ever seen:
I like it.

Graham Hemminger, "Tobacco;" *Penn State Froth*, Nov., 1915.

**GARY COOPER
AS THE TEXAN**
BY NORMAN ROCKWELL

# Tobacco,

divine, rare, superexcellent tobacco, which goes far beyond all their panaceas, potable gold, and philosopher's stones, a sovereign remedy to all diseases. *Robert Burton*

**M. and Mme Feydeau on a Sofa**
by Edouard Vuillard

# When Frédéric Chopin met George Sand

Like one of his own preludes, Chopin's first encounter with George Sand arrived at its logical conclusion with no promise of there ever being more to come. It took place in Paris in the autumn of 1836. Franz Liszt, intimate friend of both, had long wished them to meet, but Chopin had resisted. He abhorred intellectualizing in general, and by women in particular. His tastes were as delicate as his constitution. He liked his women young, beautiful, of impeccable ancestry, preferably innocent, at least discreet. George Sand was none of the above.

An introduction became inevitable, however, when Sand moved into rooms below those shared by Liszt and his mistress, Countess Marie d'Agoult, at the Hôtel de France, not far from Chopin's apartment at 38 rue de la Chausée d'Antin. Mme. Sand had therefore to be included in the small soirée at Chopin's on 5 November. Franz, Marie and George arrived together. Chopin, fragile and charming, with his aquiline nose, long, tapering fingers and aristocratic manner, found himself greeting a small (less than five foot tall) dark-haired woman clearly older (by six years) than he, who wore—as he had been warned to expect—trousers.

*It was an exceptionally relaxed evening. Chopin clowned about gently for his guests, trying not to be appalled by Sand, who puffed away at her cigar, philosophized madly, and addressed all alike in the second person singular. Tea was served.*

Later both Chopin and Liszt played. The latter exuded his usual virile charm, but in deference to the assembled company, Sand did not take her accustomed position, crouched in an ecstatic ball under the piano. She became, instead, especially when Chopin performed, cool and aloof, the detached observer. It was a role played for his benefit, but Chopin did not know that yet. "I have made the acquaintance of a great celebrity: Mme. Dudevant, known by the name of George Sand," he wrote home to his family in Poland. "Her appearance is not to my liking and doesn't please me at all."

**Nancy Caldwell Sorel**

**MEETING OF GEORGE SAND AND CHOPIN**
BY EDWARD SOREL (DETAIL)

There is nothing like tobacco;
it is the passion of all decent people;
someone who lives without tobacco
does not deserve to live.
Molière, *Don Juan*

HAVANA CIGAR MAKERS DEMONSTRATING AGAINST MECHANIZATION
(DETAIL)

Do not do unto others as you would they should do unto you.  **Their tastes may not be the same.**

**George Bernard Shaw,** *Maxims for Revolutionists*

**Im Biergarten**
by Adolph von Menzel (detail)

# It is *elegance* that is subversive, *elegance* in a world of vulgarity.
## VIVIENNE WESTWOOD

**BEAUTY PARLOR**
BY FRIDA KAHLO

# Pleasure's a sin and sometimes sin's a pleasure.

Lord Byron

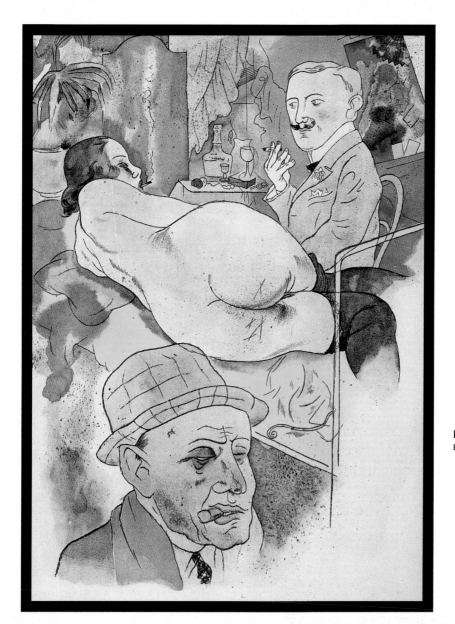

ECCE HOMO
BY GEORGE GROSZ

The saddest thing I can **imagine** is to get used to **luxury.**

**Charlie Chaplin,** *My Autobiography*

**LOUIS PASCAL**
BY HENRI DE
TOULOUSE-LAUTREC

"THE RICH MAN HAS HIS MOTOR CAR, HIS COUNTRY AND HIS TOWN ESTATE. HE SMOKES A FIFTY-CENT CIGAR, AND JEERS AT FATE."–F.P. ADAMS "The Rich Man"

**THE HEAD
OF THE FIRM**
BY ALFRED REGINALD
THOMSON

What
is
robbing
a
bank
compared
to
founding
one?

Bertolt Brecht, *The Threepenny Opera*

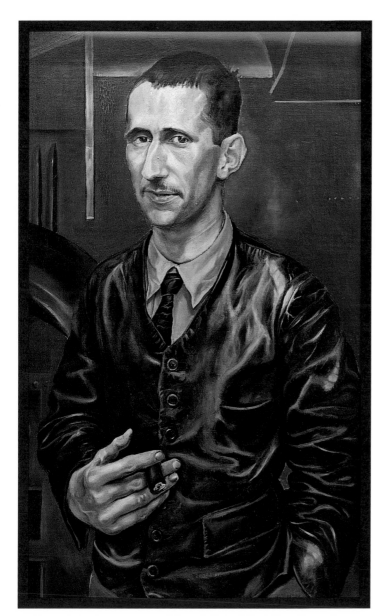

**BERTOLT BRECHT**
BY RUDOLF SCHLICHTER

# It's *easier* for a man to be *loyal* to his *club* than to his *planet*.

The by-laws are *shorter* and he is personally *acquainted* with the other *members*

E.B. White

**HAVING FUN: TIME 4AM**
BY ALBERT BECK WENZELL

Give
us
the
luxuries
of
life
and we will dispense with its necessities.  J. L. Motley

**YEATS AT PETITPAS**
BY JOHN SLOAN

By the cigars they smoke
and the composers they love,
ye shall know the texture of men's souls.

John Galsworthy, *Indian Summer of a Forsyte*

PORTRAIT OF THE ARTISTS IVAN PAVLOV, VASSILI BAKCHEIEV,
VITOLD BIALYNITSKI-BIROULIA AND VASSILI MECHKOV
BY ALEXANDRE GUERASSIMOV

# Any serious attempt to do something worthwhile is ritualistic. Derek Walcott

in *Writers at Work* (ed. George Plimpton)

ILLUSTRATION FROM SIMPLICISSIMUS
BY B. WINNERBERG (DETAIL)

Burbank crossed a little bridge
**Descending at a small hotel;**
Princess Volupine arrived,
**They were together, and he fell.**

Defunctive music under sea
**Passed seaward with the passing bell**
Slowly: the God Hercules
**Had left him, that had loved him well.**

The horses, under the axletree
**Beat up the dawn from Istria**
With even feet. Her shuttered barge
**Burned on the water all the day.**

But this or such was Bleistein's way:
**A saggy bending of the knees**
And elbows, with the palms turned out,
**Chicago Semite Viennese.**

A lustreless protrusive eye
**Stares from the protozoic slime**
At a perspective of Canaletto.
**The smoky candle-end of time**

Declines. On the Rialto once.
**The rats are underneath the piles.**
The Jew is underneath the lot.
**Money in furs. The boatman smiles,**

Princess Volupine extends
**A meagre, blue-nailed, phthisic hand**
To climb the waterstair. Lights, lights,
**She entertains Sir Ferdinand**

Klein. Who clipped the lion's wings
**And fleaed his rump and pared his claws?**
Thought Burbank, meditating on Time's ruins, and the seven laws.

# T.S.Eliot,

**Burbank with a Baedeker:
Bleistein with a Cigar**

**LA TRAVERSÉE DIFFICILE**
BY RENÉ MAGRITTE

To cease smoking is the easiest thing I ever did; I ought to know because I've done it a thousand times.   Mark Twain

THE APPEARANCE
OF WEALTH
BY J.M. FLAGG

# THE WAY UP

# IS THE

# WAY DOWN

HERACLITUS

COLLECTING
CIGAR BUTTS

I have known no man of *genius*
who has not had to pay,
in some affliction or defect either
*physical or spiritual,*
for what the gods had given him.

MAX BEERBOHM

MR ASQUITH,
"EX FORTI DULCEDO"
BY MAX BEERBOHM

Pleasure only starts
once the worm has gotten into
the fruit: to become delightful,
happiness must be tainted
with poison.

Georges Bataille, My Mother

**OUR FIRST CIGAR**
BY T. DE WITT TALMADGE

# Children have never been very good at listening to their elders, but they have never failed to imitate them.

JAMES BALDWIN

**THREE MEN, TWO CIGARS AND A BABY**
BY JAMES McMULLAN

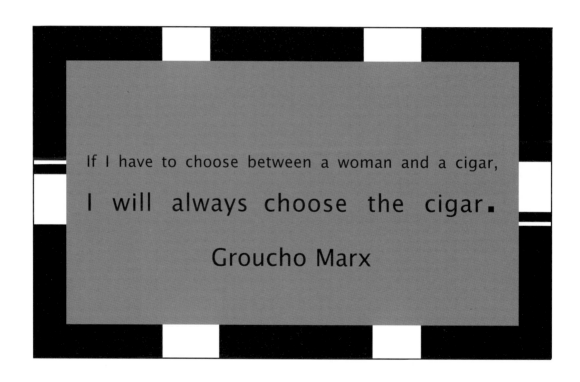

If I have to choose between a woman and a cigar,

I will always choose the cigar.

Groucho Marx

**GROUCHO MARX**
PHOTO BY
TOM ZIMBEROFF/
CONTACT

NO ONE CAN GUARANTEE **SUCCESS** IN WAR BUT ONLY **DESERVE IT.** Winston Churchill

**DOUBLE NINE:**
**ALLIED TEAMWORK WINS THE GAME**
BY CONRAD MASSAGUER

"There are men in the world
who derive as stern an exaltation
from the proximity of
disaster and ruin,
as others from
success."

WINSTON CHURCHILL, *The Malakand Field Force*

**"Confiance",**
**Winston Churchill Portrayed as an Octopus**
(Detail)

Why can't a woman be more like a man ?
Men are so honest, so thoroughly square;
Eternally noble, historically fair.

Alan Jay Lerner, *My Fair Lady*

**CIGAR-SMOKING
LADIES**
(DETAIL)

**The sweet post-prandial cigar.**   Robert Buchanan, *De Berny*

THE MAN WHO LIT HIS CIGAR BEFORE THE ROYAL TOAST
BY HENRY MAYO BATEMAN

SOCIETY DRIVES PEOPLE CRAZY WITH LUST AND CALLS IT ADVERTISING

JOHN LAHR

ADVERTISING IS THE GREATEST ART FORM OF THE TWENTIETH CENTURY

MARSHALL McLUHAN

Van Gogh circa 1889

THE DUTCH OLD MASTER OF CIGARS.

*Also ask for Rubies, Extra Senoritas and Half Coronas
from the Willem II range.*

WILLEM II · THE EXTRA MILD, EXTRA DUTCH CIGARS.

CONTEMPORARY
ADVERTISEMENT
WITH SELF-
PORTRAIT OF
VINCENT VAN
GOGH

A MAN HAS AS MUCH TROUBLE WITH HIS FIRST

# CIGAR AS

A WOMAN WITH HER FIRST BABY.

*Reflections of a Bachelor*

**DUTCH BOY
AND CIGAR**
BY NICO JUNGMAN

**I**n the ſmoke of my cigars, twenty a day,

**I** ſearched the roots of man's desire . . .

James Schevill
"Freud: Dying in London, He Recalls the Smoke of His Cigar Beginning to Sing"

**SIGMUND FREUD**
PHOTO BY
MAX HALBERSTADT

♪

♪

All art constantly aspires towards

the condition of

music.

♪

Walter Pater

♪

**EMMERICH KALMAN, COMPOSER**
BY KATRIN IDRIS

*I am **very sorry** I have not learnt to **play** at **cards.***

It is very useful in life; it generates kindness and consolidates society.

Dr. Samuel Johnson

THE GAME OF BRIDGE –
THE SALON AT THE CLOS
CÉZANNE, VAUCRESSON
BY EDOUARD VUILLARD
(DETAIL)

# Tobacco is the *opiate* of the gentleman, the *religion* of the rich.

Guillermo Cabrera Infante
*Holy Smoke*

THE PAINTER
CHRISTIAN KÖHLER
BY CARL FERDINAND
SOHN (DETAIL)

**Each** Fabrum esse suae quemque fortunae. **fate.**
man is the architect of his own

**Appius Caecus**

**PORTRAITS OF FRIENDS OF THE ARTIST**
BY ARISTIDES OECONOMO

A good novel tells us the truth about its hero;
but a bad novel tells us the truth about its author.

G.K. Chesterton

OUTLINE
of SANITY

**"The Outline of
Sanity" Satirical
Cartoon of G.K.
Chesterton**
(DETAIL)

**Strongest minds
are often those of whom
the noisy world
hears least.**

**William Wordsworth**

**SAMUEL FISCHER, PUBLISHER**
BY MAX LIEBERMANN
(DETAIL)

Anyone who's any good is obsessive.

ALAN BATES

**ELLIOTT ERWITT**
PHOTO BY MISCHA ERWITT

*M. and Mme Feydeau on a Sofa* by Edouard Vuillard, 1901. Distemper on cardboard, 18⅜ x 30⅞ in. © ADAGP, Paris and DACS, London 1996.

*Meeting of George Sand and Chopin* from *First Encounters: A Book of Memorial Meetings* by Nancy Caldwell Sorel and Edward Sorel. Copyright © 1994 by Nancy Caldwell Sorel and Edward Sorel. Reprinted by permission of Alfred A. Knopf, Inc.

*Havana Cigar Makers Demonstrating against Mechanization.* Mary Evans Picture Library.

*Im Biergarten* by Adolph von Menzel. Georg Schaefer Collection, Schweinfurt/AKG London.

*Beauty Parlour* by Frida Kahlo, 1932. Watercolor and pencil on paper, 10¼ x 8⅞ in. Collection Agustin Cristobal, Mexico.

*Ecce Homo* by George Grosz. Copyright © 1993 Gebr. Mann Verlag, Berlin.

*Louis Pascal* by Henri de Toulouse-Lautrec. Toulouse-Lautrec Museum, Albi, France/AKG London.

*The Head of the Firm* by Alfred Reginald Thompson. Bradford Art Galleries and Museums/Bridgeman Art Library, London.

*Portrait of Bertolt Brecht* by Rudolf Schlichter. Galerie Alvensleben, Munich/AKG London.

*Having Fun, Time 4 A.M.* by Albert Bell Wenzell. Photograph: Courtauld Institute of Art, London.

*Yeats at Petitpas* by John Sloan, 1919. Oil on canvas, 26¼ x 32¼ in. In the Collection of The Corcoran Gallery of Art, Washington, DC. Museum purchase, Gallery Fund.

*Portrait of the Artists Ivan Pavlov, Vassili Bakcheiev, Vitold Bialynitski-Biroulia and Vassili Mechkov* by Alexandre Guerassimov (1881-1963). Tretyakov Gallery, Moscow/Bridgeman Art Gallery, London.

*Simplicissimus* magazine illustration by B. Winnerberg. Mary Evans Picture Library.

*La Traversée Difficile* by René Magritte. Gouache on paper, 35.2 x 49.5cm. Copyright © Phototheque René Magritte-Giraudon/ADAGP, Paris and DACS, London 1996.

*The Appearance of Wealth* by J.M. Flagg. Photograph: Courtauld Institute of Art, London.

*Collecting Cigar Butts*, 1875. Engraving. Mary Evans Picture Library.

*Mr Asquith, "Ex Forti Dulcedo"* 1920, (caricature, pencil on paper) by Max Beerbohm (1872-1956). Mrs Reichmann/Bridgeman Art Library, London.

*Our First Cigar* by T. de Witt Talmadge, 1874. Mary Evans Picture Library.

*Three Men, Two Cigars and a Baby* by James McMullan. Copyright © by James McMullan.

Photograph of Groucho Marx by Tom Zimberoff/Contact. Colorific Photo Library.

*Double Nine: Allied Teamwork wins the Game*, 1944 (lithograph) by Conrad Massaguer (20th century). Franklin D. Roosevelt Library, New York/Bridgeman Art Library.

*"Confiance,"* Winston Churchill portrayed as an octopus (poster).  Lords Gallery, London/Bridgeman Art Library, London.

*Cigar-Smoking Ladies.*  Mary Evans Picture Library.

*The Man Who Lit His Cigar before the Royal Toast* by Henry Mayo Bateman (1887-1970).  Estate of H.M. Bateman/Bridgeman Art Library, London.

Advertisement for Doncella with Mona Lisa.  The Advertising Archive.

Advertisement for Willem II with Vincent Van Gogh Self Portrait.  The Advertising Archive.

*Dutch Boy and Cigar* by Nico Jungman.  Mary Evans Picture Library.

Photograph of Sigmund Freud by Max Halberstadt.  Mary Evans Picture Library.

Portrait of Emmerich Kalman by Katrin Idris.  Photo copyright © AKG, London.

*The Game of Bridge—The Salon at the Clos Cézanne, Vaucresson* by Edouard Vuillard, 1923.  Distemper on canvas, 39⅞ x 30in. © ADAGP, Paris and DACS, London 1996.

Portrait of Christian Köhler by Carl Ferdinand Sohn.  Kunstmuseum, Düsseldorf/AKG London.

Portraits of Friends of the Artist by Aristides Oeconomo.  Courtesy of Sotheby's London.

*Outline of Sanity* satirical cartoon of G.K. Chesterton.  Private Collection/Bridgeman Art Library, London.

Portrait of Samuel Fischer by Max Liebermann.  Schiller National Museum, Marbach/AKG London.

*Elliott Erwitt with Cigar* by Mischa Erwitt.  Mischa Erwitt/Magnum Photos.